Our WILD™ WORLD SERIES

Penguins

NorthWord Press
Chanhassen, Minnesota

ACKNOWLEDGMENTS
The author thanks Dr. Dee Boersma and
Dr. Wayne Lynch for sharing their time and expertise.

Photography © 2002: Stuart Klipper: cover; Wayne Lynch: pp. 4, 6-7, 10, 22, 25, 26, 29, 33, 40-41, 44; Tui De Roy/Minden Pictures: back cover, pp. 5, 13, 17, 18-19; Tom & Pat Leeson: p. 8; Robin Brandt: p. 11; Tom Walker: p. 14; Art Wolfe: pp. 20, 36-37, 39, 42-43; Frans Lanting/Minden Pictures: pp. 30, 34.

Front cover: Emperor penguins; Back cover: Adelie penguins
Illustrations by John F. McGee
Designed by Russell S. Kuepper
Edited by Barbara Harold

NorthWord Press
18705 Lake Drive East
Chanhassen, MN 55317
1-800-328-3895
www.northwordpress.com

Library of Congress Cataloging-in-Publication Data

Winner, Cherie.
    Penguins / Cherie Winner ; illustrations by John F. McGee.
       p. cm. -- (Our wild world series)
    Summary: Discusses the physical characteristics, habitat, behavior, and life cycle of penguins.
    ISBN 1-55971-811-0 (hc.) -- ISBN 1-55971-810-2 (softcover)
       1. Penguins--Juvenile literature. [Penguins.] I. McGee, John F., ill. II. Title. III.
    Series.

QL696.S473 W57 2002
598.47--dc21   2001057927

Printed in Singapore

10 9 8 7 6 5 4 3 2 1

Penguins

Cherie Winner
Illustrations by John F. McGee

NORTHWORD PRESS
Chanhassen, Minnesota

PENGUINS ARE FUN TO WATCH! You may see a group of penguins shuffling along on a tall slab of ice. Suddenly one peeks over the edge, then does a kind of belly-flop into the water. In a rush, all the other penguins follow it into the sea, making a big splash.

Penguins don't fly, but they dive deeper than any other birds, walk for miles, and climb cliffs. And even though penguins are famous for living in very cold places, they actually live in more different climates than any other family of flightless birds.

There are 17 species (SPEE-sees), or kinds, of penguins. Only two, the emperors and Adelies, spend their whole life in the Antarctic, where the winter temperature can reach −76 degrees Fahrenheit (−60 degrees Celsius). The Galapagos penguin lives near the equator. There, the temperature often reaches 100 degrees Fahrenheit (37.8 degrees Celsius). The other 14 species live on shorelines in Australia, New Zealand, South America, and Africa. The climate there is similar to the climate in the northern United States.

These Adelie penguins seem to be in a hurry to go into the water.

All penguins, like these Galapagos adults, are good swimmers and divers.

Zoologists, the scientists who study animals, divide penguins into six groups: big, little, crested, banded, brush-tailed, and yellow-eyed. They all have many things in common, such as a white belly and a black or gray back. Each species also has many differences, such as the way they raise their young and the markings on the head.

The two species of big penguins are much larger than other penguins. Emperors stand about 3 feet (1 meter) tall and can weigh up to 100 pounds (45 kilograms). King penguins are about half that size. Both have bright orange or yellow on the throat and the side of the head.

Fairy penguins are the only species in the little group. They are sometimes called blue penguins because their backs are bluish. They stand about 14 inches (35 centimeters) tall and weigh 3 pounds (1.4 kilograms).

The other kinds of penguins weigh between 5 and 20 pounds (2 and 9 kilograms) and are between 17 and 27 inches (43 and 68 centimeters) tall. In all species, males are slightly bigger than females.

This pair of king penguins have found each other after being apart while feeding. Most male and female penguins look alike.

Crested penguins have long yellow feathers above their eyes, like eyebrows. Rockhopper, macaroni, royal, erect-crested, Snares Island, and fiordland (fee-YORD-land) penguins belong to this group.

Banded penguins have a black stripe on their side, a white stripe on their cheek, or both. Galapagos (gul-OP-uh-gus), Humboldt, Magellanic (maj-uh-LAN-ic), and African penguins belong to this group.

Brush-tailed penguins have a longer tail than the others, and different patterns of black and white on the head. Adelie (uh-DAY-lee), chinstrap, and gentoo (jen-TOO) penguins belong to this group.

The yellow-eyed penguin has a yellowish stripe on its head. It isn't quite like any of the others and it lives mostly among shrubs and trees. It is in a group by itself.

The most common species in the world is the macaroni penguin. Scientists estimate there are about 19 million of them.

Emperor Penguin   King Penguin   Rockhopper Penguin   Fairy Penguin

This royal is grooming, or preening, itself. Some places are hard to reach.

All penguins have a thick coat of feathers that keeps out water and wind. Penguins need this coat to stay warm. Each penguin grooms itself for up to three hours every day keeping its feathers clean and healthy. Some species also groom their mates, and parents groom their chicks. Penguins get oil from a gland near their tail and spread it around every feather. This keeps the coat waterproof and helps protect against disease.

Their feather coat protects them from the winter chill. But in summer, penguins must cool off. They seek shady spots under a bush or in a burrow. They pant, like a dog. They hold their wings out to the side, so heat can flow away from their bodies.

Penguins are shaped like a football, plump in the middle and narrow at both ends. This shape is perfect for diving and swimming. Penguins are great at both. Penguin wings are called flippers because they are flat and stiff, like the flippers on a dolphin. Penguins swim through the water by flapping their flippers, the same way a bird flying in the air flaps its wings. They look as if they are flying underwater. Some penguins can swim as fast as 9 miles per hour (14 kilometers per hour).

Penguins spend at least half their life swimming because they only eat foods they find in the ocean. Some penguins only go a few miles out to sea. Other species swim thousands of miles to find food. Many stay at sea all winter. Fiordland penguins stay out so long, they get barnacles on their tails. Barnacles are small sea animals with hard shells that usually stick to rocks or the bottoms of ships.

After feeding, these two African penguins are heading back to their colony.

Penguins are carnivores (KAR-nuh-vorz), or meat-eaters. They consume squid, small fish such as anchovies and sardines, and tiny shrimp-like animals called krill. These sea creatures travel in huge groups called schools. When penguins find a school, they feast. One penguin can eat several pounds of food at a time. But finding these food animals, or prey (PRAY), is difficult because the schools don't stay in one place for very long. It's like having a refrigerator that is full of food but that keeps moving.

To get to where their prey are, penguins swim a few yards (meters) below the surface of the water. Sometimes they dive deeper, then they continue swimming near the surface.

When penguins find prey, they keep diving and eating for hours or even days. During one feeding trip, a gentoo penguin dove 460 times within 15 hours. It would dive, catch prey for a few minutes, come to the surface to take a breath, and then dive again.

Penguins are champion divers. They go deeper and stay underwater longer than any other birds. They usually dive 30 to 165 feet (9 to 50 meters) deep and stay down for a minute or two. But they can go 300 feet (90 meters) down and stay there for up to 6 minutes. The big penguins go even farther. The record for bird diving goes to an emperor penguin that went down 1,752 feet (535 meters) and was underwater for 18 minutes!

Penguins
FUNFACT:

Seasons in the Southern Hemisphere, where all penguins live, are the opposite of those in the Northern Hemisphere. October is early spring, and April is late fall.

This large school of fish will make a good meal
for these Galapagos penguins.

Elephant seals may peacefully share the same beach with a colony of king penguins.

Penguins hunt mainly by sight, but deep underwater, there isn't much light. Underwater, they see much better than humans. One way they find prey in the dark is by looking for flashes of bioluminescence (BY-oh-loom-ih-NESS-uns), which is light produced by animals. Many of their prey have spots that light up in the dark. These spots contain the same chemical that makes fireflies glow.

After penguins find their prey, they have to catch it. They zip one way, spin off to one side, dip and zoom and swirl in every direction. It's like an underwater dance at fast-forward speed. A trail of bubbles streams out behind them, as air that was trapped under their feathers escapes. Penguins make the prey scatter in all directions and then catch them one at a time. Because a penguin can stay underwater a long time, it might eat 100 prey on one dive.

When a penguin swallows food, it also swallows sea water. This would be poisonous for many animals, but penguins have a way to get rid of the extra salt in sea water. They have a salt gland above each eye. These glands take salt out of the penguin's blood and release it in "tears" that dribble down the penguin's bill.

When spring comes, penguins that have been at sea return to their home on land, called a colony. They go to the same colony where they were born and raised. Somehow, they know where home is.

As the penguins get closer to shore, they watch for predators (PRED-uh-torz), or enemies. Leopard seals, sea lions, and fur seals hunt for food in the water near shore, hoping to catch a plump penguin. They hide around boulders or blocks of ice in the water. Leopard seals kill more penguins than any other seal. They are quick and strong and have long, sharp teeth.

Penguins can swim for days, but they aren't fast enough to outswim these fierce predators. They need some other way of escaping harm. Traveling in a group helps, because having dozens of penguins move through the water at once can confuse a predator.

Penguins also escape by changing the way they swim. They leap out of the water like porpoises or dolphins do. This is called porpoising (POR-puhs-ing). When a penguin shoots into the air, a predator in the water can't see it. As the penguin goes back in the water, it can change direction. By the time the predator figures out where the penguin is and which direction it's going, the penguin is a long way ahead of it.

Some people think a group of swimming king penguins
looks like an underwater ballet.

Once the penguins are safely on land, they may have a long trek, or journey, to reach their colony. Penguins don't look as if they would be good at walking or climbing, but they do both quite well. Emperor and Adelie penguins often cross 50 miles (80 kilometers) or more of ice to reach their colonies. They walk part of the way and "toboggan" part of the way. This means they flop on their bellies and scoot along by pushing with their feet and flippers.

Many crested penguins must climb a tall cliff to reach their colony. Rockhoppers do this by hopping up the cliff a few inches at a time. Other crested penguins use their flippers and bill to grab onto rocks or plants and pull themselves up. The trip between the water and the colony may take them more than an hour.

Some colonies have only a few hundred penguins. Others are huge. One colony of Adelie penguins covers 200 acres (80 hectares) and is home to about half a million penguins. That is the size of a field big enough to hold two shopping malls and their parking lots, with a penguin nest every few steps across the whole field.

Strong flippers make tobogganning a quick way to travel.
An emperor's long claws also help it move over the snow and ice.

Because this macaroni colony is near the water, some of the penguins are always coming from and going to the water.

Although some colonies are huge, many are shrinking. Several species of penguins are in danger of becoming extinct, or completely dying out. Thousands of penguins are killed every year by oil spilled from ships. Others cannot find enough food. Yellow-eyed penguins are the most endangered. Only about 3,000 are still living in the wild.

If you were hiking in penguin country, the first way you would know you were near a colony would be the smell. Penguin colonies really stink! All those birds leave lots of runny guano (GWON-o), or droppings, right next to their nests. Usually they don't even bother to get up. They just point their back end out of the nest, lift their tail, and the guano squirts out. Fortunately, penguins have a poor sense of smell!

If you kept walking toward the colony, you would soon hear the penguins. They are very noisy birds. They constantly honk, squawk, trumpet, and bray. Some people say they sound like donkeys. Others think they sound like elephants or squeaky gates.

Penguins recognize each other by their voices, and they always seem to have something to say. Males and females honk as they try to get a mate. They communicate with their partner as they build a nest and care for their young. They quarrel with other penguins and warn them to stay away from their nest.

Penguins
FUNFACT:

Hundreds of fairy penguins come ashore every evening near Melbourne, Australia. On Phillip Island, bleachers are set up so tourists can watch them walk up the beach to their burrows.

Most people are surprised to learn that yellow-eyed penguins don't live near snow at all, but in the forest close to the sea.

Most penguins like to be close to other penguins, but they are also protective of their own space. Every pair claims a small territory, or area, around their nest. They peck with their bills and flap their flippers at any other penguin that steps into their territory. A penguin can hit hard enough with its flipper to knock over the intruder. To help prevent fights, each nest is just far enough from its neighbors so the penguins can't reach out and peck each other.

Yellow-eyed penguins are the only ones that want privacy when they are at the colony. They nest under bushes or in burrows far enough from other members of the colony so that they can't see each other.

Penguins often keep the same mate, especially if they were successful at raising a baby, or chick, the previous year. But the partners don't travel together during the winter, so they return to the colony at different times. The male usually arrives a few days before his mate. He finds the same nest he used the year before, and starts to get it ready for the new breeding season. He cleans it and chases other penguins away. When his mate arrives, the two greet each other with loud calls. They lift their bills to the sky and flap their flippers.

A male that doesn't yet have a mate advertises that he is looking for one. He screeches and flaps his flippers. Crested penguins, for example, also shake their heads to show off their long, bright crests, or head feathers. Sometimes two penguins fight to determine which will win a mate.

Every species has its own way of making a nest and raising chicks. Some lay their eggs in a low spot on the ground, or beneath a bush. Yellow-eyed, banded, and fairy penguins make their nests among the rocks, or they dig burrows if the ground is soft. Crested penguins use grass, leaves, and twigs to make a nest on the ground.

Penguins
FUNFACT:

Yellow-eyed penguins often stay with the same mate for 10 years or more. King and emperor penguins change partners much more often. Less than one third of them choose the same partner they had the year before.

A Magellanic burrow can be quite large. The female uses it for a safe shelter to lay her eggs and care for the newborn chicks.

The white streaks around this chinstrap nest of pebbles are guano.
Sometimes the streaks are pink or green, depending on what the penguin eats.

Brush-tailed penguins build their nest out of smooth pebbles that may be about as big as a ping-pong ball. The nest is 15 to 20 inches (38 to 51 centimeters) across and several inches (centimeters) high. A good nest keeps the egg high enough to stay dry. At the start of breeding season, the colony is surrounded by snow. As the snow melts, water streams through the nests. If an egg sits in water, the chick inside will drown. The more pebbles the parents collect, the taller their nest is and the safer their baby will be. Zoologists once found a gentoo nest that contained 1,700 pebbles!

The male penguin gathers most of the pebbles. He brings them from all over. He even steals them from his neighbors' nests, when they aren't looking. Sometimes he brings his partner an especially nice pebble as a gift.

A zoologist once did an experiment at an Adelie colony. He painted a lot of pebbles bright red and left them in a pile nearby. Within a few hours, penguins close to the pile had taken some of the red pebbles to their nests. Then other penguins noticed the pretty new pebbles and started stealing them for their own nests. Within three days, the red pebbles had spread to nests all over the colony.

As the pair works on their nest, they court each other to prepare for mating. They point their bills upward and open their flippers out to the side. They bow their heads low. They sing together, although they both have harsh voices so it doesn't sound much like singing. Sometimes they use their bills to pick ticks off of each other's face and shoulders.

The partners mate and, soon, the female lays her big white eggs. King and emperor penguins lay just one egg. All other penguins lay two eggs, but they usually raise only one chick. One egg may get broken or it doesn't hatch, or the chick is small and soon dies. Penguin parents have a hard time providing enough food for one chick. They rarely find enough food for two.

The parents sit or lie on their egg to incubate it. This keeps the egg warm so the chick inside will develop, and shades it from the sun so the chick doesn't get too hot. They turn the egg many times during the day so it warms evenly on all sides.

The parents take turns incubating. One stays on the nest while the other goes back to the sea for food. The hunting parent may be gone from the nest for a few hours to three weeks. The parent that stays on the nest doesn't eat during that whole time.

When the hunting parent comes back, the two greet each other with loud calls and excited gestures. You can tell which one just came back from the sea because it looks clean, as if it had just stepped out of a bathtub. The one that has been sitting on the nest is smeared with mud and guano. They chatter and groom each other. Then they switch places. The parent that had been hunting comes onto the nest to incubate the egg, and the other one heads for the water.

Soon these gentoo eggs will hatch and the hungry chicks will constantly beg, peck, and chirp for food from their parent.

When the weather is severe, emperors may lie down and let the snow cover them until the storm passes. Each male still protects an egg on his feet.

Penguin parents almost never leave their eggs alone. If they do, the eggs will probably be eaten by predators. Hawk-like birds called skuas (SKYOO-uhz) fly over the colony looking for a chance to snatch an egg. Crabs, snakes, and foxes also eat penguin eggs.

How long the eggs incubate depends on how big the species is. Fairy penguins only incubate their eggs for 33 days. Emperor penguins incubate theirs for 64 days, the longest of any penguin.

An emperor's life is different in other ways as well. For one thing, these birds breed in winter. That's amazing, because they live in the Antarctic, where the winters are bitter cold, windy, icy, and dark.

Also, emperors do not build nests, and the male does all the incubating. As soon as the female lays her egg, she places it on the male's feet. He has a flap of loose skin on his belly that covers the egg. It warms the egg and keeps it from rolling away. The female heads out to sea for the rest of the winter. She will hunt with other females from the colony. The male stays behind for a long, hungry winter of incubating their precious egg.

All the males in the colony huddle together to stay warm. Thousands of males stand so close that each one can rest his bill on the shoulder of the bird in front of him.

For two months, the males just stand there. They chatter quietly. They take turns being on the outside of the huddle, where it is the coldest. They don't eat at all. They use their stored body fat to stay warm in the frigid wind. A male penguin that weighs 80 pounds (36 kilograms) when he begins incubating, weighs only about 40 pounds (18 kilograms) when his job is done.

The female returns about the time the egg is ready to hatch. She is fat and healthy from spending the winter at sea. She feeds the chick and keeps it warm while the male heads for the water. He will return to help care for the chick after he has eaten a lot and gained back some weight.

Hatching, or coming out of the egg, is hard work for all penguins. The chick pokes a hole in the shell with its egg tooth, a sharp spine on the tip of its bill. Sometimes it takes the chick three days to hatch. Its parents don't help at all.

The new chick is covered with soft, fluffy feathers called down. It may be light on the belly and dark on the back, or dark all over. The baby can't stand up and its eyes stay closed for a few days.

It peeps a lot, begging for food. But it may not eat right away. The parent that is with the chick often doesn't have fresh food to give it. When the other parent comes back from hunting, it feeds the chick. It regurgitates, or throws up, some food right into the chick's mouth.

Crested penguin males stay at the nest and the females do all the hunting for the chick. In other species, the parents take turns caring for their young. While one parent goes hunting for a few days or a week, the other stays with the chick to keep it warm and protect it from skuas. These birds fly just out of reach of the adult penguins' strong bills. When they see a chick that is alone, they swoop down, grab it, and quickly fly away.

Penguins
FUNFACT:

Penguin eggs have thick, tough shells that do not break easily. An emperor egg weighs nearly 1 pound (454 grams). That is eight times as much as a chicken egg!

These rockhopper chicks are still too young to have the long, yellow "eyebrow" feathers like their parent.

This mother emperor penguin will have no trouble identifying her chick, even in such a large creche.

When chicks are several weeks old, they start to explore their habitat. In species that nest in burrows, the chicks stand outside their burrow to look around. Sometimes they gather with a few neighbor chicks. In other species, chicks leave their nests and get together in a large group called a creche (KRESH). Both parents can then go hunting at the same time.

A creche may include about 20 chicks, or as many as a few thousand. The size of the creche depends on the species and on how big the colony is. Skuas won't attack the chicks when they are in a big group like this. Huddling in a creche also helps chicks stay warm if a storm hits.

Chicks in a creche are not able to swim or hunt. They still depend on their parents for food. When an adult comes back from the sea, it calls out. Its own chick has excellent hearing and recognizes its voice and calls back. Some penguin parents run away from the creche, and the chick chases it. They might run around for half an hour. They go many yards (meters) away from the creche, to get away from the other chicks. Finally they stop running. The parent regurgitates food for the chick. If some other chick tries to steal some of the meal, the adult slaps it with a flipper.

This is a huge rookery, another name for colony. No matter how crowded it seems, there is plenty of room for these king penguins to rest and preen their feathers.

If food is plentiful, the chicks grow quickly. After a month or two in the creche, they are almost as big as their parents. Now they are too big for skuas to carry away, and they can stay warm by themselves. They lose their down and grow sleek black-and-white coats like their parents have. This change is called fledging.

While they wait for their new coat to grow in, the chicks strengthen their swimming muscles by flapping their flippers forward and backward. They waddle closer to the water and watch adults come and go. Sometimes a big wave knocks them into the sea. Then they have to swim, whether they are ready or not!

Penguin chicks face many dangers. Even in a good year, about half the chicks in a colony die before they go to sea. Storms drown or freeze them. Skuas snatch them away. Their parents get caught in an oil spill or have trouble finding food. In one very bad year, only one gentoo chick survived in a colony of 3,000 families.

More young die when they first go into the water. They don't swim well yet, and they don't know about the dangerous predators near shore. Sea lions and leopard seals catch many of them.

Penguins
FUNFACT:

Most birds have air spaces in their bones, to make them lighter so they can fly. Penguin bones are solid and heavy, to help the penguins dive deep in the water.

Adelies normally lay two eggs but often one does not survive. This parent has two chicks to feed. The parents take turns bringing food to their hungry young.

These king penguins have gathered in the colony while they wait to molt their feathers.

Young penguins that survive all these dangers join a group of adults. They are on their own now, and must find and catch their own food. Their parents have gone to sea to find food and gain back the weight they lost while rearing their chicks.

Soon the adults return to the colony to molt, or replace their feathers. All of their old, tattered feathers fall out, a few at a time, and new ones grow in their place. This takes a huge amount of energy. It also takes a long time, from 2 to 4 weeks in smaller species, and 4 to 6 weeks in bigger ones. The chicks, which just got their first coat of adult feathers, will not molt until the next year.

Molting is a hard time for the penguins. They don't eat. They don't even chatter much. Their tender skin would bruise or tear if they fought with a neighbor. So they just stand quietly as their new coat of feathers grows.

The adults are skinny and hungry when they finish molting. Then they head out to sea once more.

Emperors normally never set foot on dry land. The only time they come out of the sea is to ride on floating sea ice or breed and raise their young on the ice of Antarctica.

These kings are as much at home in the sea as any dolphin or whale.
If they are away from the colony on a long food hunt, they even sleep on the water.

Soon the air turns cold and the days grow short. Some species, like Galapagos and yellow-eyed penguins, stay near their colony all winter. They go on short hunting trips and return home within a few days. Others, like emperors and Magellanic penguins, swim the open sea all winter. They hunt and eat and grow fat hundreds of miles from the colony. They may not touch land for months. When they need to rest, they float at the surface of the water like ducks. They travel with other members of their colony, but they may not see their mates until spring, when they go home to raise a new chick.

Many young from the year before also return to the colony, but they aren't ready to breed yet. Some wait until they are 9 years old. In the meantime, they learn how to mate and raise chicks by watching the older birds.

That seems like a long time to wait before raising offspring of their own, but wild penguins can live for about 20 years. Those young birds will be part of a crowded, noisy, smelly, thriving penguin colony for many years to come.

Penguins
FUNFACT:

Some penguin colonies are more than 4,000 years old, some are about 100 years old, and others are nearly new. Gentoos move to a fresh place every few years.

Internet Sites

You can find out more interesting information about penguins and lots of other wildlife by visiting these web sites.

www.animaldiscovery.com	Discovery Channel Online
www.antarctic.com.au	Antarctic Adventure
www.enchantedLearning.com	Enchanted Learning
www.kidsplanet.org	Defenders of Wildlife
www.nationalgeographic.com	National Geographic Society
www.nwf.org	National Wildlife Federation
www.pbs.org/edens/patagonia	PBS (Public Broadcast System)
www.penguin.net.nz	Penguins in New Zealand
www.seabirds.org/penguins	International Penguin Conservation Work Group
www.tnc.org	The Nature Conservatory
www.wcs.org	Wildlife Conservation Society
www.worldwildlife.org/fun/kids.cfm	World Wildlife Fund

Index

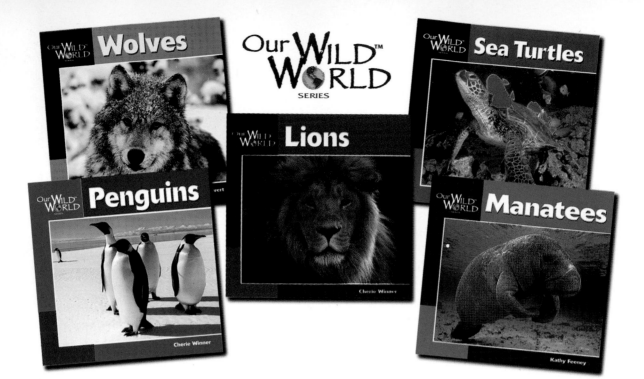

Paperback titles available in the Our Wild World Series:

BISON
ISBN 1-55971-775-0

BLACK BEARS
ISBN 1-55971-742-4

CARIBOU
ISBN 1-55971-812-9

COUGARS
ISBN 1-55971-788-2

DOLPHINS
ISBN 1-55971-776-9

EAGLES
ISBN 1-55971-777-7

LEOPARDS
ISBN 1-55971-796-3

LIONS
ISBN 1-55971-787-4

MANATEES
ISBN 1-55971-778-5

MOOSE
ISBN 1-55971-744-0

PENGUINS
ISBN 1-55971-810-2

POLAR BEARS
ISBN 1-55971-828-5

SEA TURTLES
ISBN 1-55971-746-7

SEALS
ISBN 1-55971-826-9

SHARKS
ISBN 1-55971-779-3

TIGERS
ISBN 1-55971-797-1

WHALES
ISBN 1-55971-780-7

WHITETAIL DEER
ISBN 1-55971-743-2

WOLVES
ISBN 1-55971-748-3

See your nearest bookseller, or order by phone 1-800-328-3895

NORTHWORD PRESS
Chanhassen, Minnesota